THE POND BOOK

Karen Dawe

Illustrated by Joe Weissmann

A Somerville House Book

WORKMAN PUBLISHING, NEW YORK

Workman Publishing
 Company, Inc.
708 Broadway
New York, NY 10003-9555

**Library of Congress
Cataloging-in-Publication
Data**
Dawe, Karen
The Pond Book/
by Karen Dawe;
illustrated by Joe Weissman.
p. cm
"A Somerville House book."
ISBN 1-56305-921-5
1. Pond Ecology—Juvenile
literature. 2. Pond fauna—
Juvenile literature. 3. Ponds—
Juvenile literature. [1. Pond
ecology. 2. Pond animals. 3.
ecology. 4. Frogs. 5. Toads.]
I. Weissman, Joe, ill. II. Title.
QH541.5.P63D38 1995
574.5'26322—dc20

95-3289
CIP
AC

Manufactured in the
United States of America

First printing May 1995

10 9 8 7 6 5 4 3 2 1

Special thanks to:
Rick Dowson, Grande River
Conservation Authority,
The Royal Ontario Museum,
and Rama Chengalath
at the Canadian Museum
of Nature, for scientific
consultation.

For my folks,
Rene and George Hagen,
with love.

Contents

Be a Wetland
  Explorer 5
Pond and Tank Tips .. 6
What Are
  Wetlands? 10
The Food Chain 12
Water Is More
  Than Wet! 14
Creature Key 16

Look on the
Surface 20
Pond Lily 22
Duckweed 23
Pond Snail 24
Surface Bugs 26
Fisher Spider 28
Pond Birds 30

Look in the
Water 32
Bladderwort 34

Giant Water Bug 35
Backswimmer 36
Water Boatman 38
Diving Beetle 39
Flash! It's a Fish! 40
Turtle 42
Snake 43
*Mammals of the
  Wetlands* 44

The Lives
of Frogs and
Toads 46
The Difference
  Between Frogs
  and Toads 48
Food on the Go 50
Masters
  of Disguise 51
Courtship and Egg
  Laying 52
Metamorphosis 54

Tree Frogs 56
...and Other
  Frogs 58
Spadefoot Toads 60
...and Other
  Toads 62

Look on the
Bottom 64
Cattail 66
Leech 67
Clam 68
Crayfish 69
Water Scorpion 70
Dragonfly Larva 72
Damselfly Larva 73
Caddisfly Larva 74
Mayfly Larva 75
Salamander 76
Save the Wetlands ... 78

Checklist 80

Be a Wetland Explorer

Every pond, big or small, is a miniature world bustling and teeming with diggers and divers, floaters and fliers, slitherers and swimmers, waders and wallowers.

The Pond Book will introduce you to this fascinating freshwater world of plants and animals and will help you discover the living laboratory right at your feet. Look under leaves and on stems, scoop up water with your tadpole tank or dig in the mud and examine creatures up close with the pond wand. Search for a bug with a built-in snorkel, a spider that goes fishing, even a plant that eats animals!

As you observe and investigate, you'll learn what makes those plops and splashes, how the pond snail clings to the water surface and why only female mosquitoes bite. This field guide can help you solve these mysteries and more.

Somewhere near you, a pond or lake or stream or marsh is out there full of surprises. What are you waiting for? Grab your tadpole tank, tuck your book inside and explore!

Pond and Tank Tips

1 Expect to get wet! Wear rubber boots or old sneakers to protect your feet from biting insects and sharp objects. Carry a pack and stuff it with lunch, a notebook and a pencil. If you're very organized, pack an extra set of dry clothes wrapped in a plastic bag.

2 Explore by looking first. Sit silently on the shore and watch the activity around you. Listen. Let the animals get used to your presence. Then, as you begin your investigations, move slowly.

3 Look on plant stems and search on or under submerged or floating leaves. Many small animals eat plants or lay their eggs on them. Others swim in the water or hide in the vegetation.

Never go near the water alone, and always make sure an adult knows where you are. Wear a life jacket, especially if the water is deep.

4 Use your tadpole tank to hold any animals you find, and look in your book to identify them. If you can't find them here, check the Creature Key to find out what kind of animal it is, then look it up in a more comprehensive field guide.

5 The lid of your tank is the pond wand. Use the pond

wand as a strainer or dip net. Gently pull it through the water or the muddy bottom and let the water drain as you lift it. The pond

Do Not Touch!

Watch for this sign beside some of the animals in this book. Big or small, many are predators that bite or sting, so be careful when you catch them. Always use your pond wand to scoop an animal into your tank. Don't hold it in your hand—you might hurt the animal, and it could hurt you.

wand can also help you capture creatures and transfer them to your tadpole tank.

6 Look at tiny plants and animals close-up with the magnifying lens in the center of the pond wand.

7 Be gentle. Always handle plants and animals kindly. Remember, you are a giant to them.

8 Try to make the pond animals comfortable while you observe them. If they're water creatures, make sure there is plenty of water in your tank. If they're air breathers, keep the tank dry. Make sure the animals are cool and protected from the sun. Too much heat can kill.

9 Keep a list of all the plants and animals you find. Make notes about where they live, what they do and how many you see. Draw pictures to help you remember their shapes, markings and colors.

10 Return every creature to the pond after you've observed it. Try to put it back exactly where you found it. Leave the habitat—and the plants and animals living there—as you found them.

What Are Wetlands?

Wetlands are places where water collects into lakes, ponds, streams, rivers, marshes and swamps. The wetlands in this book are freshwater ecosystems—complex communities of plants and animals interacting with one another and their surroundings. There is a lot of action in a wetland, where plant and animal organisms live, find food and shelter, mate, raise young and eventually die. Each plant and animal makes its living in a different way, but all are dependent on one another and on their watery environment.

In a pond, plants and animals are everywhere—floating on the surface, swimming in the water or crawling in the mud. Lakes are large, deep, cool on the bottom and warm on top. Plants

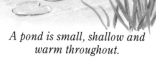

A pond is small, shallow and warm throughout.

Marshes are large, muddy and grassy areas.

LOOK FOR bubbles rising from the mud. Marsh gas and sulfur gas are given off by microscopic creatures as they decompose, or break down dead plants and animals. Marsh gas is odorless, but sulfur gas smells bad.

and animals live all along the shoreline. Marsh plants are rooted in the mud while their leaves reach above the quiet, shallow water. Plants grow along the banks of rivers and streams. Animals burrow in the muddy bottom, attach themselves to rocks, or swim through the water.

Rivers and streams are moving waters that flow swiftly.

11

The Food Chain

All organisms need food for energy to survive. How these organisms obtain their food determines whether they are producers or consumers. The transfer of food or energy from a producer to a consumer is called a food chain. Each plant and animal is a link in a food chain, and each food chain begins with a plant.

Plants are PRODUCERS. Using a gas called carbon dioxide, water and energy from sunlight, plants produce their own food in a process called photosynthesis.

Animals are CONSUMERS. They cannot make their own food, so they get energy by eating other things. They eat plants or other animals that have eaten plants.

The chain doesn't end with consumers. When an animal dies, its body falls to the bottom of the pond and becomes food for microscopic organisms called bacteria and fungi. Bacteria and fungi are DECOMPOSERS. Living mainly in the mud, they break down dead plants and animals and release nutrients back into the water to be used by plants—as the food chain begins again.

> **Every single food you eat first comes from a plant—even ice cream! It's made from milk, which comes from cows, who eat grass.**

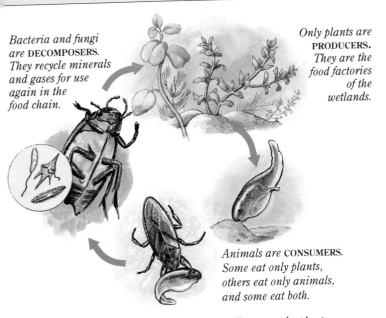

Bacteria and fungi are **DECOMPOSERS.** *They recycle minerals and gases for use again in the food chain.*

Only plants are **PRODUCERS.** *They are the food factories of the wetlands.*

Animals are **CONSUMERS.** *Some eat only plants, others eat only animals, and some eat both.*

Every food chain begins with a plant. For example, plants are eaten by tadpoles, who are then eaten by beetles . . .

13

Water Is More Than Wet!

Believe it or not, fresh water is not just water! It's an ever-changing soup of dissolved gases and minerals, tiny plants and animals, and small bits of dead and decaying organisms. Ocean water has about 100 times more minerals than the fresh water you find in a pond. Plants and animals live in either salt water or fresh water, but usually not in both.

Oxygen

Most living creatures need oxygen to break down food and release its energy. You breathe oxygen from the air, but many underwater animals and plants absorb oxygen that is dissolved in the water. Most of the oxygen comes from plants, which give off this gas when they make their food. Without this dissolved oxygen, few plants and animals could survive in the water.

Why worry about acid rain? Because plants and animals die in an acid environment. The acid can dissolve calcium and other minerals in their bodies.

14

Temperature

Because water temperatures change more slowly than air temperatures, water plants and animals are protected from the rapid changes of the outside air. Even in winter, beneath a blanket of ice, many animals are active while others dig into the mud to hibernate. Some plants and animals die in the cold, but their seeds or eggs can survive the winter to grow in the spring.

Minerals

Minerals, dissolved from surrounding rocks, are vital to life in the water. Calcium is one of the most important minerals; snails and clams build their shells with it and fish build bones with it. Water rich in minerals is called alkaline and supports a large community of plants and animals. In contrast, acid water has few minerals . . . and few living things.

Plankton and Detritus

Waters rich in oxygen and minerals teem with microscopic animals (zooplankton) and plants (phytoplankton). Phytoplankton is the first link in pond food chains. Pond water is also rich in detritus—bits of dead organisms that settle to the bottom mud. There, it is broken down by decomposers or eaten by bottom-dwelling creatures.

Creature Key
A Guide to Invertebrates, or Animals Without Backbones

GROUP	WORMS	MOLLUSKS
Example	*Leech*	*Snail*
Limbs	None	None
Body Covering	Soft, thin skin	Soft, skin-like mantle, usually covered by shell
Notes	Most freshwater worms breathe through their skin; some have gills. Many worms burrow in the bottom mud.	Mollusks are soft-bodied creatures protected by a shell. Bivalves, such as clams, have a shell made of two valves, or parts, joined in the middle. Univalves, such as snails, have a one-piece shell. Some mollusks, such as slugs, don't have a shell.

ARTHROPODS: SPIDERS	CRUSTACEANS	INSECTS
Fisher spider	*Crayfish*	*Water strider*
8, jointed	Variable, usually 14, jointed	6, jointed; some also have 4 wings
Hard external skeleton	Hard external skeleton	Hard external skeleton
Male spiders are smaller than females. Both spin silk from special glands, called spinnerets, at the end of their abdomen. Liquid silk is squeezed out of the spinnerets and hardens into a tough, elastic strand.	Most crustaceans live in water. Because the hard skeleton is on the outside of the body, crustaceans can grow only by molting, or shedding their skeletons.	An adult insect looks very different from its young form, called larva. Insects change from larvae into adults through a process called metamorphosis.

Creature Key *A Guide to Vertebrates, or Animals With Backbones*

GROUP	FISHES	AMPHIBIANS
Example	*Sunfish*	*Salamander*
Limbs	Variable, fins	4 legs or none
Body Covering	Usually scales	Soft, moist skin
Notes	Fishes have a line of sensors along each side of the body, called a lateral line. These sensors are sensitive to all kinds of vibrations and pressures in the water. A fish feels the movement of other animals through its lateral line.	Amphibian larvae live in water, breathe with gills and eat plants. They look completely different from the adults, which live on land, breathe with lungs and eat meat. For more on this change, see page 54.

REPTILES	BIRDS	MAMMALS
Turtle	*Belted kingfisher*	*Muskrat*
4 legs or none	4: 2 wings and 2 legs	4 legs, or 2 arms and 2 legs
Scales	Skin and feathers	Skin and hair
Reptiles have dry scales covering their bodies and are cold-blooded. Since they take on the temperature of their surroundings, they bask in the sun to warm up. If they get too hot, they retreat to the shade.	Birds are warm-blooded, egg-laying animals that are covered with feathers. Male birds sing to defend their territory and attract mates. Males are usually more brightly colored than females.	All mammals are warm-blooded, have hair and feed their young with milk made in the mother's body.

Look on the Surface

Many plants and air-breathing animals actually live on the surface of the water. Wherever air and water meet, molecules of water cling together and form a thin elastic film called SURFACE TENSION. This surface film can support the weight of small, lightweight animals and plants. To a tiny insect this surface film can be as solid as a brick wall is to you!

Watch the activity on the surface. Look for little dimples in the water where a water strider stretches the film with its legs or where a mosquito larva pokes its breathing tube into the air.

Pond Lily

Pond lily

APPEARANCE: The rounded, leathery leaves of pond lilies floating on the pond surface often cover large areas, shading and cooling the water on hot days. Their thick, twisting roots are anchored firmly in the bottom mud while yellow, cup-like flowers poke above the pond's surface.

NOTES: Like many water plants, pond lilies have air spaces in their leaves and stems to help them float. Look for frogs, dragonflies, spiders and other pond animals that may rest on the flat leaves. Feel the upper surface of a lily pad. The waxy coating protects the leaf from becoming waterlogged in the rain or dried in the sun and wind.

LOOK FOR a lily pad with a circular hole about the size of a quarter, and gently turn over the leaf. You may find the missing piece attached with silken threads to the leaf's underside. This "pocket" is the underwater work of the moth caterpillar, which slices and spins to make its watery hideout.

Duckweed

APPEARANCE: Duckweed is one of the smallest flowering plants. Each duckweed plant has a single, flat, round or oval body, smaller than your little fingernail, with one or more long rootlets dangling down directly into the water. Occasionally in the summer, small flowers grow along the plant's edge.

NOTES: Ducks and other water birds eat duckweed, and many small animals spend their whole lives in the thick carpets of duckweed. As colder weather approaches, duckweed stores more food and sinks to the bottom of the pond. In the spring, after the duckweed has used up the food and is lighter, it floats to the surface.

Duckweed

MINI-PROJECT

Scoop some duckweed into your tadpole tank and use your magnifying lens to look for plants that appear to be joined together. Here a new plant is budding from the parent and will eventually pinch off and float away. Observe how each rootlet balances the plant in the water.

Pond Snail

APPEARANCE: Pond snails have a soft body covered by a smooth, thin, one-piece shell that grows in a spiral shape. They are mollusks. Their shells come in various shades of brown, gray or black. Some snails are as long as your first finger. The snail's body is tucked into the shell, and when the snail moves, you can see its flat, muscular foot.

FOOD: Algae and bits of plants that are scraped off with the radula—a file-like tongue covered with rows of tiny teeth.

NOTES: Hanging upside down, pond snails actually cling and crawl along the under-side of the surface film! These snails have a lung and come above the the surface of the water to breathe air. Other kinds of snails have gills and absorb oxygen from the water.

Pond snail

POND PROJECT

Look for pond snails creeping just under the water surface, across the pond bottom, on the underside of lily pads or on stems and leaves of other plants close to the shore. Pick up the snail and put it in your water-filled tank.

The snail pulls its body inside its shell to protect itself, but if you are patient, it may extend its muscular foot. Its head, with two tentacles, is at the front end of the foot; its mouth is on the underside. Look for a dark eyespot at the base of each tentacle.

Watch the underside of the snail's foot as it slowly crawls along the bottom or side of your tank. Mucus glands on the bottom of the snail's foot lay down a highway of slime for it to glide over. The body movement flows from the rear of the foot toward the front and pushes the snail forward.

During dry summer periods or in winter, the slime hardens over the opening of the shell and seals the snail safely inside until the pond is liveable again. Other kinds of snails have a "trapdoor" that closes over the opening.

Surface Bugs

Insects are everywhere! Look for these three common insects on the pond's surface.

Water strider

• The WATER STRIDER skates across the water. Its long middle legs are used like oars to pull it over the water while the back pair guide it in the right direction. The water strider's short front legs hold on to captured insects while it sucks out the victim's juices. Make sure your tank is emptied of water if you catch this insect. Water striders can drown if they are trapped under the surface film.

• The WHIRLIGIG BEETLE is so named because it whirls around and around on top of the water surface. It uses its paddle-shaped back legs to spin in circles in search of food. This shiny black insect is an expert underwater swimmer, too. When alarmed, it dives, carrying a bubble of air to use as a breathing supply. The whirligig's eyes are divided in two: the top half sees above the water while the bottom half looks into the depths.

Whirligig beetle

Mosquito larvae

• The female MOSQUITO lays rafts of eggs on the surface film and the larvae hatch into the water. Each larva pushes a breathing tube through the water to the air above and hangs head down from the surface film by its tube. If disturbed, a larva closes its breathing tube and wriggles to the bottom of the pond by flipping its abdomen back and forth.

Only a female mosquito bites. Her body needs the protein in blood to make eggs. As she inserts her needle-like beak into your skin, she injects a blood thinner to keep your blood flowing. That is what makes the mosquito's bite itch.

Adult mosquito

Fisher Spider

APPEARANCE: Eight long legs spread the weight of the fisher spider's hairy body and allow it to walk across the surface film as eight eyes search for unwary prey. The fisher spider is brown and has a light stripe along each side of its body.

Fisher spider

FOOD: Insects, tadpoles, small fishes.

NOTES: Instead of building a web to trap food, this fast-moving hunter races across the water to capture insects. The fisher spider even goes fishing by using its own foot as bait! Slowly it moves one foot back and forth on the water surface. When a curious fish is lured close, the spider dives into the water and catches it.

POND PROJECT

Be sure to empty the water from your tank before you capture a fisher spider—air breathers can drown in rough water. When you find a fisher spider resting on a floating leaf, use your pond wand, not your hands, to scoop it gently into the tank. Most spiders are harmless to people, but you may be allergic to the bite.

Use your magnifying lens to look at the fine hairs covering the spider's body. When it dives into the water, air is trapped in the hairs close to the body. The spider breathes the trapped air through open-ings under its abdomen and can stay underwater as long as its air supply lasts.

To find out if the spider is a male or a female, look between the first legs and the mouth for a pair of small, leg-like palps. If the palps are narrow to the tip, you've found a female; a male's palps have a round ball on the end. A male is also a lot smaller than a female.

Female palp   *Male palp*

Pond Birds

Many birds find food, shelter and nesting places at a pond. Here are three birds you might see and hear.

Common yellowthroat

• A PIED-BILLED GREBE can slowly sink underwater, leaving only a faint ripple in the surface. But if alarmed, the "hell diver" quickly dives below the surface. With its legs set far back on the underside of its body, the grebe is an expert on the water but clumsy on land. If you hear a series of loud, bubbly whoops echoing across the water, look for a grebe.

Pied-billed grebe

Belted kingfisher

• The BELTED KINGFISHER hovers in the air before diving headfirst into the pond to grab a fish in its bill. Then it flies up to a high perch to eat its catch. You may hear a rattling call before you see this big-headed bird dive with a splash into the water.

• The energetic COMMON YELLOW-THROAT sings "witchety, witchety, witchety-witch" from the marsh plants to warn his enemies and defend his territory. Try calling to the warbler with a "psh-psh-psh" sound.

MINI-PROJECT

Sit silently on the shore and listen for the songs and calls of the birds around you. Often you'll hear the song before you see the singer. Use the song as a guide to help you track down the bird.

Look in the Water

The world between the water surface and the pond bottom is called the water column. Some of the animals that live here spend their whole lives underwater and are expert swimmers. Some are plant eaters, chewing chunks out of leaves or devouring the plankton that surrounds them. Others are meat-eating hunters on the move, darting quickly in search of prey or lurking among the plant stems and leaves, waiting for their food to swim past. Many animals are only visitors to the pond, land dwellers that come to the water to lay their eggs or feast on the abundance of food.

Bladderwort

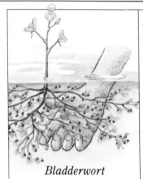

Bladderwort

APPEARANCE: Feathery clusters of this meat-eating plant float below the water's surface and are rootless. The bladderwort has many narrow leaves and is covered with small bladders, or sacs, that grow along the branching stems.

NOTES: Most plants absorb nutrients from the soil, but rootless plants need to find nutrients in a different way. The bladderwort catches tiny animals. Each tiny bladder is a snare and has a trapdoor surrounded by sensitive hairs. If an animal touches a hair, the trapdoor pops open, suck-the animal in. Then the trapdoor snaps shut and the bladderwort slowly digests its prey.

MINI-PROJECT

Lift some bladderwort into your empty tadpole tank and see how it collapses into a limp mass without water to support it. Use your magnifying lens to look at the bladders among the leaves. The black spots on the inside of the bladders are the remains of tiny animals.

Giant Water Bug

Giant water bug

APPEARANCE: The flattened, oval body of the giant water bug is dark brown or green and may grow to be the length of a new crayon. Its two sturdy front legs are used to snatch food, and the four rear legs, flattened and fringed with hairs, are used for swimming. The giant water bug breathes through a short breathing tube that pokes out from the end of its abdomen. Note its large overlapping wing covers. Another pair of wings is hidden underneath.

FOOD: Insects, fishes and other animals up to the size of salamanders.

NOTES: Watch out! The giant water bug is the largest and fiercest bug you'll find in the water. It devours anything and everything that comes within reach. Look for it clinging, head down, to underwater plants, waiting for dinner to swim near before stunning its prey with a poisonous sting. It can bite you, too!

35

Backswimmer

APPEARANCE: The backswimmer is a small, greenish insect that earned its name because it swims upside down—on its back! Its oar-like back legs stick straight out from its body and "row" the bug leisurely along. A silvery bubble of air glistens on its dark belly, allowing the backswimmer to breathe underwater. Note its big red eyes.

FOOD: Insects, tadpoles, small fishes. The backswimmer bites its prey with needle-like mouthparts and then sucks out the juices.

Backswimmer

POND PROJECT

Be sure to use your pond wand to catch this insect; the backswimmer is a meat eater and can give you a painful bite. Place the insect in your water-filled tadpole tank and let the water calm down.

As the backswimmer swims, you can see its six legs: the two short forward pairs are used for holding on to underwater plants and grasping small animals.

Watch how the bug rows with both long hind legs at the same time, pauses, and then rows again; on each pause it floats upward, rear end first. Its light-colored back is V-shaped like the bottom of a boat, and so cuts smoothly through the water.

While you watch, the backswimmer might float to the surface and hang head down. The tip of its abdomen pushes through the surface film and air is trapped in the body hairs. As the insect submerges, it carries the glistening bubble of air on its belly and sides for underwater breathing.

Water Boatman

Water boatman

APPEARANCE: The water boatman looks similar to a backswimmer, but it swims right-side up! This small insect is covered in tiny gray-and-black stripes, sometimes tinged with yellow. Flattened back legs stick far out from its body and look like long oars rowing through the water.

FOOD: Small animals and plants.

NOTES: Water boatmen anchor themselves to plants by grasping a stem with their long middle legs; when they let go or stop swimming, they float upward. Boatmen break the surface headfirst and capture air along the hairs on their back and belly. Tiny hairs on their long back legs lie flat and slip easily through the water. But as the legs move backward, pushing against the water, the hairs spread out to form a flat paddle—and the boatman zips away.

Diving beetle adult

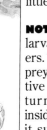

Diving beetle larva

APPEARANCE: The big, oval-shaped, blackish diving beetle may grow longer than your little finger. Its back legs, covered with bristly hairs, row rapidly as it chases after food.

FOOD: Insects, tadpoles, small fishes and other little animals.

NOTES: Both adult and larva are expert hunters. The larva grabs its prey and injects digestive juices as it bites, turning the victim's insides into liquid. Then it sucks up its soupy meal!

 MINI-PROJECT

Look at the shiny, hard wing covers that meet in a line along the middle of the diving beetle's back. Like all insects, the beetle breathes through pores called spiracles. When it dives, it carries air under its wings close to the spiracles. Watch as the beetle surfaces, hangs head down, and lifts its wing covers to trap air under them.

Flash! It's a Fish!

Freshwater fishes come in all shapes and sizes. Three small fishes of the shallows are shown here.

• Tiny, fast-moving DARTERS zip through the water, suddenly stop, and then race ahead again. You can see them rest on the bottom with their fins outstretched. Look along slow-moving edges of streams or lakes to find darters. Pale females attach their eggs to the underside of rocks, in gravel, or on algae and plant stems. The male stays with the eggs as they develop; he removes debris and fans the eggs to circulate the water and to assure plenty of oxygen.

• The SUNFISH is a hand-size, rounded fish with a flattened, brightly colored body. Watch for greens, reds, oranges, and blues flashing in the

Darter

Sunfish

sunlight as it forages for insects and their larvae. Many sunfishes may swim and nest together among plants along the shore.

• Finger-length STICKLEBACKS have sharp spines along their greenish backs. In the spring, males turn almost black, and each builds a hol-low, round nest of algae, grasses and twigs on or near the bottom. After a female lays her eggs in the nest, the male chases her away and looks after the developing young by himself.

Stickleback

 MINI-PROJECT

Catch a fish! Lower your tadpole tank into the water behind the fish and gently shoo it inside with the pond wand. Watch how the fish opens and closes its mouth and gill covers when swimming. As its mouth opens, water is sucked inside, then pushed out over the gills when the fish closes its mouth. The fish breathes by absorbing oxygen from the water as it flows over its gills. Sometimes you can see the red gills beneath the gill covers.

Turtle

APPEARANCE: Turtles are covered above and below by a hard shell made of bony plates. The rounded upper shell is often a colorful green or brown with patterns or splotches of red, yellow or orange. This reptile has no teeth. Instead it uses a hard beak to rip food into pieces.

FOOD: Mainly plants and seeds; some kinds of turtles eat worms and other small animals.

NOTES: Turtles are cold-blooded, like all reptiles, and need to bask in the sun to raise their body temperature. Although they spend a lot of time in the water, turtles come to land to lay their leathery eggs. Not all turtles pull their head and legs into their shell for protection. Some will snap and bite with their powerful jaws; others release a terrible-smelling scent.

LOOK FOR the overlapping plates of a turtle's shell. Within each plate are many circles within circles. The plates form rings of growth similar to those of a tree, a clamshell or a fish's scales.

Snake

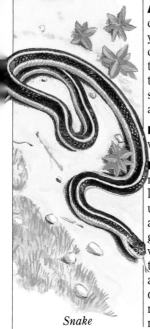

Snake

APPEARANCE: A snake is a legless reptile, covered in dry scales from head to tail. Oranges, yellows, reds, browns, blacks and greens are common snake colors, often in stripes or patterns. Some can grow to be as long as you are tall. Most snakes will bite to protect themselves, and some water snakes are poisonous and deadly.

FOOD: Worms, slugs, fishes, frogs and mice, which are swallowed whole, headfirst.

NOTES: Snakes swim with the same side-to-side motion they use on land. Some even dive underwater and wait among the plants to grab their dinner. In winter, when temperatures drop, snakes find a safe den and go into a deep sleep called hibernation. Many snakes may share one den.

LOOK FOR molted snake skins wedged between rocks or grasses along the water's edge. A snake rubs its snout until the skin splits. Then it slides its body forward, turning the skin inside out.

43

Mammals of the Wetlands

The three common mammals shown here frequently leave their five-toed footprints along the shore.

• The RACCOON uses its sensitive front feet to feel for food under rocks and plants in the water. When prey is caught, the raccoon often dips it back into the water again, almost as if washing the food. Raccoons are usually loners but females keep their kits, or young, with them over the winter.

Beaver

Raccoon

• BEAVERS are the master architects of the wetlands. They build dams of mud, branches and twigs, and turn streams into ponds. And they do it all with four paws, one tail and two front teeth!

• In the middle of a cattail clump a MUSKRAT sits up, on its haunches mouse-like, and crunches on juicy cattail shoots. When the muskrat swims, its long, thin, hairless tail is used as a rudder.

LOOK FOR signs of these three mammals near the pond.

If you spot a hollow tree with a hole, tap on the trunk. A masked raccoon might peek out at you.

Pointed, gnawed-on stumps of small trees around the water's edge are a sure sign of a beaver at work. Look closely at a stump for the beaver's chisel-like tooth marks.

Look over the water for a muskrat's house—a dome-shaped lodge built of cattails and other water plants plastered together with mud. Wait patiently and you might see a muskrat, too. Or look on land between the small muskrat footprints for the drag mark made by the tail.

Muskrat

The Lives of Frogs and Toa

Frogs and toads are amphibians, which means they live two lives. An amphibian's first life is in the water, where it hatches, eats plants, breathes through gills and looks more or less like a fish. But when it grows up, its body completely changes for its second life on land, where it eats meat and breathes with lungs.

Frogs and toads look alike, but there are a few differences. Frogs live near water, have a slim body covered with smooth skin and have long legs with webbed feet for jumping and swimming. Toads live away from water, have dry, warty skin and short legs with no webbing. Toads are more suited for walking and hopping on dry land. Yet, there are warty-skinned frogs who live on land and there are toads with smooth skin. The word frog is often used to mean both frogs and toads.

FROGS

Tympanum eardrum

Slim body, with smooth, moist skin

A male frog or toad has a vocal sac, which amplifies his mating song.

Long, muscular legs

Webbed hind feet

Frogs and Toads

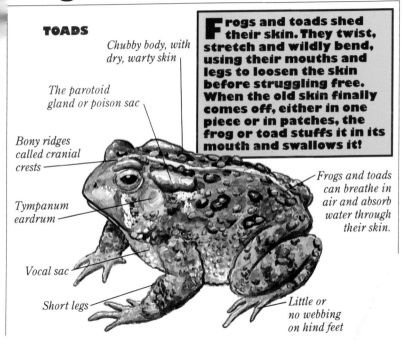

TOADS

Chubby body, with dry, warty skin

The parotoid gland or poison sac

Bony ridges called cranial crests

Tympanum eardrum

Vocal sac

Short legs

Frogs and toads shed their skin. They twist, stretch and wildly bend, using their mouths and legs to loosen the skin before struggling free. When the old skin finally comes off, either in one piece or in patches, the frog or toad stuffs it in its mouth and swallows it!

Frogs and toads can breathe in air and absorb water through their skin.

Little or no webbing on hind feet

Food on the Go

Frogs and toads are carnivores and will eat almost any creature that can fit in their big mouths—bugs and worms, mice and birds. They even eat tadpoles! Frogs eat a lot of food when it's available, but they can go a long time between meals.

A frog's sticky tongue is attached to the front of its mouth and can be quickly flipped out to catch a moving meal. Once the prey is caught, the frog whips its tongue back into its mouth and swallows. When a frog swallows, it has to close its eyes because the pressure of the eyeballs helps to force the food down.

If an animal moves, a frog can catch it with its muscular, sticky tongue. The frog responds to the [mo]tion of the animal, [not] the animal itself. [If it doe]sn't move, it [won't be] eaten.

A flip of a frog tongue is fast and precise.

Masters of Disguise

To avoid becoming dinner, frogs and toads have unique ways to protect themselves against predators.

Coloring camouflages them so they blend in with their surroundings. If they can't be seen, they can't be eaten.

Toads have a poison gland behind each eye that can ooze a milky, bitter poison. Any predator that picks up the toad in its mouth

A puffed-up toad can look dangerous.

gets a nasty, sickening surprise and drops the toad quickly.

Many frogs defend themselves by puffing up to look bigger and scarier.

A wild leap is a frog's split-second way to escape from a hungry predator. A frog can dive to the bottom of the pond, kicking up a muddy cloud as it hides among the plants.

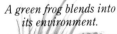

A green frog blends into its environment.

Courtship and Egg Laying

In springtime or after heavy rains, when the ice is melting from the edges of the pond, crowds of male frogs and toads fill the air with their croaky songs.

These mating calls attract female frogs and toads and, like birds, you can identify different species of frogs and toads by their songs.

When a male finds a mate, the female lays her eggs in the water and the male releases sperm to fertilize them. A female frog can lay up to 30,000 eggs!

A male frog fertilizes the eggs as they are laid.

Most frogs lay clusters of eggs; toads lay their eggs in strings.

Each dark egg is covered with a jelly-like coating. The eggs cling together and may stick to underwater plants, or float to the top of the pond where they are warmed by the sun. There the eggs grow and change shape from tadpoles to frogs through metamorphosis.

LOOK FOR masses of small, jelly-like eggs floating in the water or stuck to plants and twigs.

Use the magnifying lens in your pond wand to look closely at the eggs. Don't try to scoop the eggs into your tank or you may damage them. Through the clear jelly you can see dark spots in the middle. These are developing tadpoles. Can you see any of them wriggling?

Metamorphosis

Amphibians are among the magicians of the wetlands! Like insects, the young change into adults through metamorphosis, a process in which the body form and structure changes.

This change is astonishing. In spring, frogs and toads return to the pond to lay masses of eggs. These eggs hatch into plant-eating, water-dwelling tadpoles that change in 2 to 16 weeks into meat-eating, land-living adults.

1. The tadpole grows inside the jelly-like coating and wriggles out of the spawn.

2. The feathery gills slowly become covered by skin and the hind legs grow. The tadpole now breathes through the inside gills.

Spiracle

3. As the tadpole's front legs develop, its tail starts to shrink. This tiny frog with a tail is called a froglet. The froglet eats tiny animals and must swim to the surface to breathe.

POND PROJECT

Carefully collect three or four tadpoles in your tadpole tank. Remember, in the early stages they are *very* fragile. Use your magnifying lens to look at the tadpoles. If a tadpole has feathery gills on each side of its neck, it has just hatched. Within two or three weeks, a fold of skin will grow over the gills.

Look on the left side of the tadpole's body for the small opening called a spiracle. As water flows over the tadpole's covered gills, oxygen is absorbed. Then, the water is pushed out through the spiracle. You might also see the intestines coiled inside its transparent belly.

If you catch a tadpole with only hind legs, look near the spiracle for the starting bump of the left front leg. As the front legs grow, the tail starts to be absorbed into the tadpole's body.

If your tadpole looks like a small frog with a tail, it is almost ready for life on land. Watch how it swims, holding the front legs near its body and pushing with the hind legs. When you are finished observing your tadpoles, remember to return them to the pond.

Tree Frogs

The frogs on these pages have mastered the ability to live in trees. Tree frogs have special sticky pads on their toes, which are perfect for clinging to smooth leaves, slippery bark and skinny branches. All tree frogs are small. A large one may grow to the length of half a crayon.

Pacific tree frog

Chorus frog

• The PACIFIC TREE FROG is a small and sprightly tree climber with large toe pads. It avoids danger by changing its body color to match its surroundings. No matter what color it is, it will always have a dark line from its nose to its shoulder. Listen for a loud, two-chirp call from the shrubs and low branches along the Pacific coast.

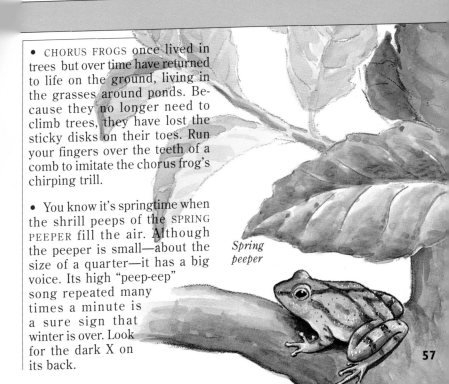

• CHORUS FROGS once lived in trees but over time have returned to life on the ground, living in the grasses around ponds. Because they no longer need to climb trees, they have lost the sticky disks on their toes. Run your fingers over the teeth of a comb to imitate the chorus frog's chirping trill.

• You know it's springtime when the shrill peeps of the SPRING PEEPER fill the air. Although the peeper is small—about the size of a quarter—it has a big voice. Its high "peep-eep" song repeated many times a minute is a sure sign that winter is over. Look for the dark X on its back.

Spring peeper

57

...and Other Frogs

Jump! It's a frog! All frogs are expert jumpers. Some frogs are smaller than your thumb, and others are as large as a football. They are colored in greens, browns or grays with bright splashes of red, green or yellow. Here are three frogs you might see and hear in and around the pond:

• The BULLFROG is the largest frog in North America and stays near the water year-round. Bullfrogs have huge appetites and eat almost anything that moves and is smaller than they are. However, the bullfrog is not an active hunter. He sits and waits for his prey to appear. That is also how he finds a mate—he just waits for her to come along. You may see a large male floating belly-up in the water, showing off his yellow throat to the females. Listen for his deep "jug-o-rum" song.

Bullfrog

LOOK FOR the tympanum to find out if a bullfrog is male or female. If it is a male, the eardrum will be larger than his eye. A female's is the same size as her eye.

Green frog

• The LEOPARD FROG is as big as your hand and is covered with dark spots outlined in a lighter green. This frog has two back ridges from its nose to its hind legs. When startled, the leopard frog zigs one way and zags another toward the water. This frog's song is like the "putt-putt-putt" of a motorboat.

• The GREEN FROG looks like a small bullfrog but has a white belly and a metallic green line on its upper lip. Green frogs warm their bodies by sunning themselves along pond banks. Look for two ridges on the green frog's back from the eye down to the hump. Listen for a low, muffled grunt like the sound of a loose banjo string and you've heard the song of the green frog.

Leopard frog

Spadefoot Toads

Spadefoot toads are expert diggers. They have hard black ridges on their back feet to help them burrow backward into soft, cool sand where they can rest during the day and keep their skin from drying out.

• The WESTERN SPADEFOOT is grayish green and blends into its grassy home. It is found in sandy soil near ponds or under rocks. The western spadefoot toad comes out to find food only at night or after it rains. If you handle this toad, its poison may make you sneeze.

Western spadefoot

In the winter, most frogs hibernate. Because they are cold-blooded, their body temperatures are as cold or as warm as the air around them. To survive cold weather, they burrow into mud or soil and sleep until their world warms up in the spring. If they couldn't escape the cold, they would freeze.

• The EASTERN SPADEFOOT is found east of the Mississippi. Like all spadefoot toads, they breed and grow up very quickly. After a heavy rain, these toads take advantage of the temporary puddle-ponds. The females can lay up to 20,000 eggs at a time, and an egg can develop into a young toad in only two weeks.

Plains spadefoot

Eastern spadefoot

• The PLAINS SPADEFOOT lives in grassy areas where the soil is soft and easy to dig. It spirals its way backward until it is completely covered. Its song sounds like a short "quack." Look for a large bump between its eyes.

Toads live on dry ground away from the pond. They are quiet during the day and hunt at night for bugs, worms and spiders. Most toads have bumpy skin that feels dry to the touch, and all of them have a large poison gland behind each eye. The toads on these pages are stocky and squat, colored in earth tones— grays, red-browns or greens.

• The most common toad in North America is the warty AMERICAN TOAD. Look for one or two warts in each dark spot on its back. The American toad, with its long high song, may be a welcome visitor to your garden as it eats countless insects.

> **Y**ou can't get warts from toads! But the toad's bumps, like the glands behind each eye, are sacs of poison that can make an enemy sick. If you handle a toad, keep your hands away from your mouth and eyes—the poison may make you sick, too. Wash your hands if you've handled a toad.

American toad

Western toad

• The GREAT PLAINS TOAD lives in prairies in the West. To attract a mate, the male calls out in a harsh screech that lasts 10 to 15 seconds. He makes this song by inflating a vocal sac under his chin. When inflated, the vocal sac is bigger than the toad's head!

Great Plains toad

• The WESTERN TOAD, found west of the Rockies, walks instead of hopping and hunts its food by sitting and waiting for it to come along. If you frighten a western toad, it might try to run away or it might puff itself up to scare you away! Listen for the faint "cheeping" of a chick and you may have found a western toad.

63

The bottom of the pond is crawling with life. Many creatures probe through the muddy pond bottom scavenging for food, while others search for prey or hide among the thick tangle of plant stems and roots.

Some animals spend their entire lives in the depths, while others spend just their early stages on the bottom before growing into adults that crawl on land or fly in the air. The pond bottom is also a place where you can find all sorts of animals that periodically dive down to escape from danger and hide.

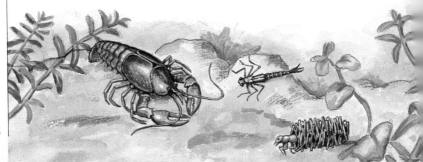

Cattail

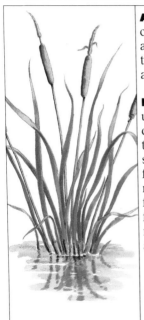

APPEARANCE: Cattails are known by their characteristic cigar-shaped brown flower spikes and long, narrow flat leaves. Rooted securely in the bottom mud, clumps of cattails grow high above the water into the air.

NOTES: Cattails grow from a special type of underground stem called a rhizome. Rhizomes creep outward in all directions from the root of the parent plant under the mud. Each rhizome sprouts, and eventually adult cattails create dense foliage that attracts many animals. If you find cattail stems lying flat in a circle over the mud, you've discovered a muskrat dining spot.

LOOK FOR the fuzz on the flower spike. Each piece of fuzz acts as a tiny parachute attached to the end of one seed. Over the winter thousands of seeds cling to the flower spike, then scatter on the wind in spring.

Cattail

Leech

Note the strong suckers.

APPEARANCE: A leech is a flattened worm with a large sucker at the rear end of its body and a smaller sucker at the mouth end. These invertebrates come in greens, grays, browns or blacks, often with stripes or patterns of bright colors. Some leeches are small, but others can grow as long as your foot.

FOOD: Some suck blood; others eat meat.

NOTES: Watch out for this bloodsucker! Using its suction-cup mouth to hold on to an animal, the leech bites with three sharp teeth and injects a painkiller. It sucks blood until it's full and then lets go. A leech swims by wriggling its body up and down in a wavelike motion.

MINI-PROJECT

During the day, look under submerged logs and rocks for leeches. Use your pond wand to scoop a leech into your tank. If the leech attaches its suckers to the side of the tadpole tank, use your lens to look at the suckers as it inches its way along the inside of the tank wall.

Clam

Clam

To move or dig into muddy and sandy bottoms, the clam extends a narrow, muscular foot from between the valves.

APPEARANCE: The two valves of this mollusk's shell are often covered in a flaky, brown skin and are joined by a leathery hinge. The clam's soft body is hidden inside the protecting shell. Most freshwater clams are small, but some are as long as your hand.

FOOD: Plankton and detritus.

NOTES: To breathe and eat, the clam draws water into its body through a short, hose-like siphon that sticks out of its shell. The siphon is divided into two tubes: one draws in water and food; the other pumps out water and waste. As the clam grows, it builds its shell by adding calcium, filtered out of the water to the valve's outer edge. During winter, the shell growth slows down. This results in tiny rings on the clam's shell.

LOOK FOR the trail the clam leaves behind as it slowly drags its shell along.

Crayfish

Crayfish

APPEARANCE: A crayfish is a crustacean. Like its lobster relatives, it has a shell, antennae and ten legs. The first pair of legs are large, with strong pincers for grasping and shredding food, and the smaller legs are used for moving. A crayfish can grow as long as your hand and is usually the same color as its habitat, splashed with bright color.

FOOD: Mainly plants but also anything that comes within reach.

NOTES: Most "crawdads" hide during the day under plant debris and rocks. If frightened, they shoot backward by flipping their abdomen and three-piece tail fan forward.

MINI-PROJECT

Use your pond wand to catch a crayfish. You'll have to be fast! Gently put the crayfish into your tadpole tank and look on the underside of its long abdomen for five pairs of tiny "legs" called swimmerets. A female carries her eggs glued to the swimmerets. Use your lens to find her newly hatched young clinging to them.

69

APPEARANCE: The long, stick-like water scorpion can grow to be the length of a new crayon. It has two long, semi-circular tubes sticking out from the end of its abdomen; these fit together to make one long, round breathing passage. The water scorpion's two front legs are thicker than the other four and are used for catching food. Don't be fooled by the water scorpion's innocent appearance. It is a predator and will bite.

Water scorpion

FOOD: Insects, insect larvae, tadpoles.

NOTES: The water scorpion clings motionless to plant stems or lurks in the bottom mud. It is not a scorpion at all, but an insect related to backswimmers and water boatmen. It has adapted to a life surrounded by water. Out of water the water scorpion seems clumsy; underwater, its long body and legs are delicate and graceful.

POND PROJECT

You'll have to be a pond detective to find a water scorpion in the pond's shallows. Disguised as a twig, it clings motionlessly to submerged stems and blends in perfectly with its surroundings.

Look at the end of the water scorpion's body to find its long breathing tube. The insect holds on to water plants with its long legs and pokes this "snorkel" through the surface film to the air above.

Now look at the water scorpion's small head and two large eyes. In front of the eyes is a pointed beak deadly to a water scorpion's prey. This hunter hides among the water plants, watching for prey to come near. Quickly, it shoots out its two front legs and grasps its dinner. Then it pierces the insect with its beak and sucks up the juices, leaving an empty shell behind.

Put your tadpole tank into the water so the insect can return to the water plants. Blink and it's gone, blending back into the vegetation.

Dragonfly Larva

Dragonfly larva

The dragonfly adult flies around the pond, darting over the surface, scooping other flying insects into a basket made by its two front legs. Listen for the rattle made by its wings.

APPEARANCE: The chunky dragonfly larva is often covered with algae and blends in with its surroundings. Its green or dark gray body may be hairy or smooth. Rows of gills are hidden inside its abdomen.

FOOD: Insects, insect larvae, worms, tadpoles, small fishes—even other dragonfly larvae.

NOTES: A dragonfly larva is a fearsome predator that hides among plants, waiting to ambush unwary prey. Its long, sharp lower lip folds between its legs and shoots out lightning-fast to stab a small animal, then it whips the food to its mouth where the prey is crushed. If threatened, the larva shoots water out the end of its abdomen and rockets away.

Damselfly Larva

Damselfly larva

The adult damselfly folds its two pairs of wings lengthwise over its back when resting.

APPEARANCE: Drab green, gray or brown, the damselfly larva is about as long as your thumb. It has three pairs of legs and three delicate gills at the tip of its slender abdomen.

FOOD: Worms, insects, insect larvae, tadpoles, other small animals.

NOTES: A damselfly larva must shed its skin often as it grows into an adult damselfly. When the air-breathing adult is fully developed, it climbs out of the water on a plant stem, splits its skin along the top of its back and struggles out. Look for shed skins of damselfly and dragonfly larvae attached to plants in the shallows.

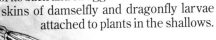

Caddisfly Larva

Caddisfly larva

After the caddisfly adult struggles from its larval case, it must dry its hairy wings to harden them before they can be used for flying.

APPEARANCE: A caddisfly larva actually builds a house for itself! Inside a hollow case made of small twigs, leaves or pebbles, the larva has a dark head and a soft, pale-colored body and legs.

FOOD: Algae and other plants, animals, detritus.

NOTES: Inside its house, the caddisfly larva continually moves its body to keep water flowing over its thread-like gills. When metamorphosis is finished and it's time for the adult to emerge, the larva leaves its house behind. Then it wriggles to the surface and clings to a stem.

MINI-PROJECT

Collect several caddisfly larvae in your tank. Watch a larva crawl partially out of its case and jerkily pull it along. If you move, the larva may zip back inside its house.

Mayfly Larva

Mayfly larva

Adult mayflies never eat! Most live only a few hours and spend their entire lives swarming over the water, mating and laying eggs before they die.

APPEARANCE: The drab gray or brown mayfly larva has two or three tails at the end of its body. It has large eyes on its head and a strong claw on each of its six feet. Pairs of flattened, feathery gills along the sides of its abdomen beat constantly to move water around its body.

FOOD: Algae and other plants, animals, detritus.

NOTES: From spring into early summer, the mayfly goes through a two-part change from a larva into an adult. First, the larva floats to the surface, quickly struggles from its casing and flies away. These mayflies are not yet adults; they are called sub-adults. Usually within a day, the sub-adult sheds its outer covering too, and out climbs the true adult. Look for shed skins attached to tall stems and leaves above the pond.

Salamander

APPEARANCE: The shy adult salamander has a slender body, a long tail and smooth, slippery skin; some have four legs, others are legless. These brown, yellow, red or black amphibians are often striped or spotted. Most can fit into your hand, but some salamanders can grow to two feet long! Like frogs and toads, salamanders begin life in the water and grow up to live on land. The larva lives in water and resembles the adult but has a large tail fin and feathery gills on the side of its neck.

FOOD: Earthworms, insects, insect larvae, clams, snails, slugs, frogs, tadpoles, even mice.

Salamander adult

Salamander larva

POND PROJECT

Look for a larva.

Carefully lift underwater plant debris from the pond bottom to find a salamander larva. When you spot one, quickly scoop up the animal with your pond wand and put it gently into your water-filled tadpole tank.

Use the magnifying lens to look at the feathery gills on the side of its neck. As the salamander swims, the gills remove oxygen from the water. The broad tail fin gives this animal a fish-like appearance. As the larva changes into an adult through metamorphosis, the gills and tail fin shrink and are absorbed into the body.

Look for an adult.

Adult salamanders live in moist places on land and return to the water to lay their jelly-like eggs. Look in the leaves along the shore for the air-breathing adult. Although harmless, larger salamanders may try to bite, and some release a smelly liquid from their skin glands.

Sometimes a predator bites off a salamander's toe, tail, or leg. If your animal is missing a tail or leg, don't worry. Salamanders can regrow lost limbs within a short time. Look closely and you might see a stubby replacement already growing.

Save the Wetlands

Where would we be without wetlands? They not only store all the earth's fresh water, but they also control flooding, modify the weather and even filter pollution from the water.

Wetlands are bustling with life. They are thriving communities of plants and animals. But despite their importance, wetlands—and the species that make wetlands their home—are rapidly disappearing. As cities grow and expand, wetlands are drained, filled and developed to make way for office buildings, houses, factories and shopping centers.

All across North America, people are working to keep the wetlands safe. No matter where you live, you can help! Here are some ideas:

1. Adopt a local wetland. Encourage your friends and teacher to choose a nearby wetland for a special biology classroom. You can write articles and draw pictures for your school or local newspaper about your wetland and its inhabitants.

2. Be a wetland watchdog. Keep an eye on the health of your wetland. Make a journal and write down all the different kinds of plants and animals that you see. Do frogs live there? If not, why not? Ask at your library for books that will help you learn about the signs of pollution.

3. Join organizations such as The Nature Conservancy, The National Wildlife Federation or The National Audubon Society. They are continually working to save wetlands.

All over the world, frogs and toads are mysteriously disappearing. Some scientists think that ultraviolet light from the sun may be killing the amphibians, others believe pollution is the cause.

4. But most important, learn all you can about the wetlands. Ask questions about the plants and animals that live there and how they work together to form these unique ecosystems. Wetlands are worth it!

Checklist

Check off the plants and animals *you* find as you explore the wetlands.

☐ Backswimmer	36
☐ Beaver	44
☐ Beetle, Diving	39
☐ Beetle, Whirligig	26
☐ Bladderwort	34
☐ Bullfrog	58
☐ Caddisfly	74
☐ Cattail	66
☐ Clam	68
☐ Crayfish	69
☐ Damselfly	73
☐ Darter	40
☐ Dragonfly	72
☐ Duckweed	23
☐ Frog, Chorus	56
☐ Frog, Green	58
☐ Frog, Leopard	58
☐ Grebe, Pied-billed	30
☐ Kingfisher, Belted	30
☐ Leech	67
☐ Lily, Pond	22
☐ Mayfly	75
☐ Mosquito	27
☐ Muskrat	45
☐ Raccoon	44
☐ Salamander	76
☐ Snail, Pond	24
☐ Snake	43
☐ Spider, Fisher	28
☐ Spring Peeper	56
☐ Stickleback	41
☐ Sunfish	40
☐ Toad, American	62
☐ Toad, Eastern Spadefoot	60
☐ Toad, Great Plains	62
☐ Toad, Plains Spadefoot	60
☐ Toad, Western	62
☐ Toad, Western Spadefoot	60
☐ Tree Frog, Pacific	56
☐ Turtle	42
☐ Water Boatman	38
☐ Water Bug, Giant	35
☐ Water Scorpion	70
☐ Water Strider	26
☐ Yellowthroat, Common	31